THE ALTERNATIVE KNOT BOOK

Dedicated to Geoffrey Budworth

THE ALTERNATIVE KNOT BOOK

DR HARRY ASHER
M.A., Ph.D

NAUTICAL

Published by Nautical Books
an imprint of
A & C Black (Publishers) Ltd
35 Bedford Row, London WC1R 4JH

ISBN 0 7136 5950 5

A CIP catalogue record for this book
is available from the British Library.

By the same author
The Seeing Eye
Experiments in Seeing
Photographic Principles and Practices
Muscle and Bone
A New System of Knotting

Principal illustrator Phil Vernon

Photoset by Rowland Phototypesetting Ltd
Bury St Edmunds, Suffolk
Printed and bound in Great Britain by
The Bath Press Ltd, Bath

Contents

Acknowledgements

I gratefully acknowledge the continuous supportive help I have received over several years from Mr Geoffrey Budworth, present President of the International Guild of Knot Tyers and Editor of its Quarterly Journal, also from fellow Guild Members Mr Desmond Mandeville, Mr Ettrick Thomson, and many others. Especially valuable information has been contributed by Mr M. R. Parsey of Marlow Yacht Ropes, who taught me much that I had been unable to find from books.

I warmly thank my friends Annie and Bob Lee in Guernsey for the trouble they have taken to put me in touch with Mr Hilary de Baugy, a farmer, who from his own great experience has assured me that to use a Cow Hitch is not the way to tether a cow. (See page 26.)

Foreword

Although the new synthetic ropes introduced after the last war marked a notable improvement in quality, unfortunately there has been no corresponding rise in the knowledge or skill of people concerned with rope work; indeed there has been a regrettable tendency to rely on a variety of clips, brackets and other forms of gadgetry.

The present book aims to reverse this tendency. It describes a basic set of 75 knots, from which the reader may extract a selection suited to his tastes and needs. Many new knots*, and some new methods of tying old ones, are described in terms of a new system developed within the last three years. It will give old hands something new to think about, but it should also prove helpful to the beginner because it can now be seen that many different knots hitherto regarded as unrelated now fall into place in an orderly system. This feature makes knots both easier to learn and more readily remembered; most of the new ones can be recorded in the form of a concise formula.

The book starts from the very beginning, and no knowledge at all on the part of the reader is assumed.

Harry Asher
79 Oakfield Road
Selly Park
Birmingham B29 7HL
England
Phone 021-472 0365

* New knots are indicated with an asterisk throughout the book.

1 Rope

To get under way, start by taking a good look at a piece of ordinary three-strand rope; it is laid up right-handed (left-handed rope is hard to find). In Fig. 1 observer A on the left sees each strand receding from him clockwise. What is perhaps surprising is that observer B on the right, who is looking the other way, also sees the strands receding from him clockwise. Both observers therefore agree that the rope is laid up right-handed.

Thus the *sense* of the lay, whether left- or right-handed, has nothing to do with where it is placed or how it is viewed, but is a property of the rope itself. The same thing applies to screws; a right-hand thread is normal, but screws with left-hand threads are available for special purposes (for example extracting right-hand screws which have got stuck).

1

A   **B**

The Structure of Rope

From about 3000 BC until the time of the Second World War, rope was made from the natural fibres of manila, hemp, sisal, flax, cotton or coir. Because the fibres are of limited, as opposed to continuous, length they are known as 'staple' fibres. To form them into rope they had to be twisted tightly together to grip by friction. To make *right-laid rope*, small bundles of fibres were twisted together to make *right-hand yarns*; these were then twisted together the opposite way to make *left-hand strands*, which in turn were laid up to form *right-laid rope* (see Fig. 1a). It is the alternate direction of the twists that holds the rope together and gives it strength.

To get the feel of this counter-twisting, unlay one of the three strands of a piece of normal right-laid rope for about a foot; now wind the strand back into the empty groove. To make a neat job you will find that you have to maintain a tight left lay of the yarns in the strands to enable the strand to fit tightly in the right-handed groove in the right-laid rope.

There is, however, one considerable defect in the traditional method of making rope from staple fibres. Twisting is essential to confer strength, but this strength is not more than about thirty per cent of what it would be if the fibres were continuous and ran straight without twist all the way along the rope. Twist puts a tax on the strength it confers.

Synthetic Rope

Nylon, used for the first rope made of synthetic material, made its dramatic appearance towards the end of the Second World War, and all but brought to an end a stretch of 5,000 years during which natural plant fibres held sway. Several other kinds of synthetic rope followed showing some differences, but they all share certain common characteristics. Size for size they are lighter, stronger and cheaper than ropes made from natural fibres; they do not rot if left wet; they take a range of colours well, and colour coding on board ship for instant recognition of ropes of different function is a universal boon. Coding with one or more differently coloured yarns visible on the surface allows manufacturers to mark their different products.

All synthetic ropes except Kevlar™ have melting points between 120°C and 250°C. Kevlar™ is the latest and strongest synthetic material; it does not melt, but chars at around 350°C. In a chandlery, ropes other than Kevlar™ are cut to a required length with an electrically heated knife, thus sealing the end and leaving a sharp edge. The user, however, will cut the rope with an ordinary sharp knife, and then melt the end with a cigarette lighter or on an electric ring; both give a clean melt which is then carefully rounded off with a moistened finger (ouch!). A match, a candle, or night light tend to deposit soot.

The new feature of all the synthetics is that they can be made in continuous lengths. It is therefore not essential for the filaments to be twisted together for them to cohere, and rope can be produced in a wide variety of patterns.

There are broadly two types:

Laid-up synthetics can be made in the old way by first chopping the filaments into discrete lengths or *staple filaments*, and then with successive twists in opposing directions producing first yarns, then strands, and finally rope. But why chop? The reason is that continuous filaments give a smoother rope with a different feel, and knots hold less well in it. However, much synthetic rope is made from continuous filaments, and the smoothness is accepted. But here too there must be some twist, because unorganized strands of loose filaments would not hold together.

Plaited or braided synthetics are the other main type, though with many varieties. As laid down officially the two terms have identical meaning, though 'plaited' usually describes solid plaits of four or eight strands, while 'braided' applies to forms with a sheath of 16 or more strands surrounding either an inner hollow braided core or a solid core of parallel, or only slightly twisted, filaments.

Thus the laid-up synthetic ropes gain strength only from the excellent properties of the synthetic materials, while the braided forms gain further through avoidance of the loss of strength through twisting.

Laid-up rope made from the relatively thick multifilaments (above 0.002 ins diameter) twisted tightly, give excellent wear resistance, but tend to be stiff; knots may be awkward to tie and may hold less well. Plaited or braided rope made from the thinner 'polyfilaments' (less than 0.002 ins diameter) can be astonishingly flexible and a delight to handle, though wear resistance is less good and knots may tend to jam.

Nylon (polyamide) is strong and gives the greatest stretch (except for shock cord). Because of this it is useful for towing either a boat or a vehicle. Stretch is a property which is desirable in a whipping twine, but Nylon is not used for this purpose because it is too strongly affected by the u.v. radiation of sunlight.

Terylene™/**Dacron**™ (polyester) gives very little stretch, and still less if 'pre-stretched'. It is nearly as strong as nylon and is widely used for sheets and halyards; also for whipping twine.

Polypropylene though not as strong as nylon or Terylene™ is a popular general purpose rope, suitable, for example, for mooring warps. The special feature is that it floats, so saving loss through sinking but adding danger of entanglement in the propeller. Being cheaper, the slight deficit in strength can be compensated for by going one size larger.

Polythene (polyethylene) is weaker than any of the ropes above, and is not held in high esteem.

Kevlar™ (aramide) is distinctly stronger than any of the other materials, but it is expensive and sensitive to the action of ultraviolet rays. It is used mainly as a core of parallel, or only slightly twisted filaments protected by an outer braided sheath. The extra cost can be, to some extent, offset by use of rope a size smaller.

Shock Cord consists of fine elasticated yarns encased in a durable sheath. It will stretch to nearly double its length and with a hook at each end is handy for holding things in place on deck or on a luggage rack.

Some Breaking Loads (lbs)

Diameter	6mm	8mm	10mm
Kevlar™ Core	2640	<u>5510</u>	8460
Nylon, 3-strand	1650	2980	4590
Terylene™, 3-strand	1250	2250	3500
Terylene™, 16-plait	2200	3750	<u>5730</u>
Polypropylene, 3-strand	1100	2000	3000
Polythene, 3-strand	880	1540	2400
Manila, 3-strand	670	1260	1660
Hemp, 3-strand	670	1120	1570
Sisal	560	1060	1400

Note the large gain in strength conferred by an increase in diameter of 2mm; for laid-up ropes, strength is approximately proportional to cross sectional area. The two underlined figures 5510 and 5730 show that despite the effect of diameter, the 8mm Kevlar™ core rope is almost as strong as the 16-plait 10mm Terylene™. The Table also brings out the superiority of the synthetic materials, and the figures for the two kinds of Terylene™ demonstrate the advantage of the plaited over the laid-up form. Finally, remembering that 1 ton = 2240 lbs and that 1 inch = 25.4mm, one can only be impressed by the enormous strength of modern ropes.

Coiling a Rope

A rope that is repeatedly coiled incorrectly can become sadly tangled and kinked, and can even reach the extreme state where the only way to clear it is to tow it astern. Few people understand the cause of this ancient trouble, but the following experiments show what happens.

Experiment 1. To Make a Perfect Coil
Lay out a foot or so of right-laid rope dead straight on a flat surface. I am using 6mm white polypropylene, but almost anything will serve. With a felt pen make a straight line of dots or dashes along the top (Fig. 2), and push a nail or toothpick vertically through the end dot.

Straight line of dots or dashes

Turn 360°

Hold the rope firmly with the left hand, and with the right hand apply one 360° rotation with the lay (clockwise). This will loosen the lay, and the line of dots now makes one complete spiral turn (Fig. 3). Next, while keeping the nail upright, slowly bring the two hands together. Although you did not deliberately make a turn, you will in fact have produced one.

2

3

Now examine the dotted line once more and note – possibly to your surprise – that it no longer forms a spiral, but lies accurately on the circumference of a circle (Fig. 4). The two separate actions, the twist and the approach of the hands have combined to reproduce the simple curl of an elephant's trunk coiled to put food into his mouth.

The conclusion sounds contradictory: *For the coil to be untwisted, one full twist with the lay must be applied for every turn wound on.*

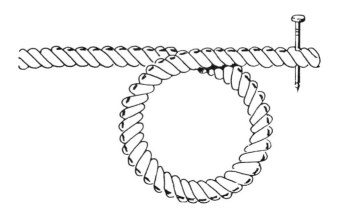

4

Experiment 2. The Perfect Coil Yields Twisted Rope

Starting from the position reached at the end of Experiment 1, separate the two hands to straighten out the rope. From what we now know it is no surprise to find that the spiral has been reformed, and all the original twist restored.

Trivial though this experiment may seem, it does demonstrate that a 'perfect' coil made to contain no twists would prove far from perfect in use, and would produce one complete twist for every turn run out from it.

Experiment 3. The Twisted Coil Yields Perfect Rope

Starting with the rope straight, while keeping the nail upright, try to make a single small clockwise turn. The rope resists strongly and must be forced. Notice that the lay has been tightened, and although the nail did not rotate or deviate from its vertical setting, the dots now once more form one complete spiral turn! (Fig. 5).

While keeping the nail vertical, pull the rope out straight, and notice that no trace of twist remains. *For rope to come off untwisted there must be one 360° twist per turn in the coil.*

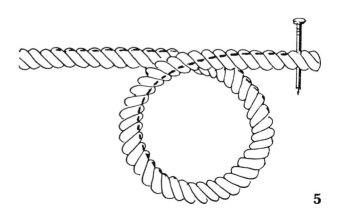

5

What to Do?

It is clear that there must be twists somewhere: either one per turn in the coil, and none in the rope run out from it; or none in the coil, and one per turn in the rope taken from it; or a compromise with a smaller amount in each.

At first it would seem that to live with this problem all we have to do is to make the coils sufficiently large, because with coils of the normal size of a few feet in diameter the effects produced by the previous experiments are so small as to be quite hard to demonstrate. Why, then, is there ever a serious practical problem? The explanation must be that if one combined coiling and uncoiling can leave a small residual twist, frequent repetition will produce a cumulative effect which can leave the rope in a sorry state.

The traditional advice is to coil clockwise and make a 'slight twist' with the lay to loosen it. This approach is really a watered down version of Experiment 1, where a perfect coil yielded a twisted rope. Indeed, the twist is admitted by a leading authority Brion Toss, who writes:

> "When the coil runs out, all those little twists have to go somewhere, and if you coil clockwise . . . right-laid three-strand rope can unlay a bit to absorb them."

Readers may like to minimize or even omit the slight twists with the lay, and so make a less tidy coil. It will include up to one full twist per turn against the lay, but will deliver rope with minimum or even zero twist; and with zero twist there can be no cumulative effect. But with circular coils there is no perfect solution, because *there is a real conflict between tidiness and twist.*

Finishing a Coil

Complete the upstroke of your last clockwise turn, take the rope down a short way on the other half and then across the coil in front as you start to wind a few tight turns upwards round both halves. Push a bight through the gap as shown, then fold it back over the top (Fig. 6). You can finish thus, or by taking the end back through the gap.

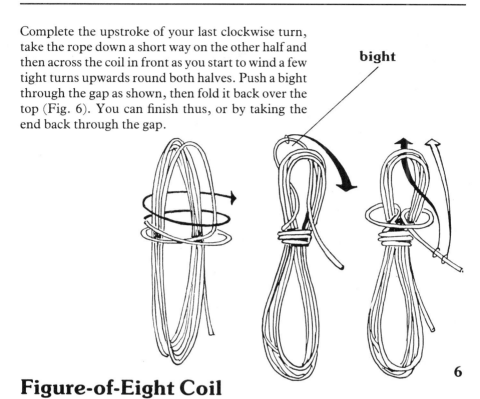

bight

6

Figure-of-Eight Coil

Coiling as a Figure-of-Eight almost eliminates all problems of kinking, but the coil does not hold its shape unless laid on deck. With light rope the coil may be quickly made by lifting the bight with each wrist alternately.

The End of the Rope

A Thumb Knot tied in the end will prevent unravelling, but it makes an awkward lump. Heat sealing for synthetics has already been described. For ropes of natural fibre good quality, slightly stretchy insulating tape can be effective.

2 Hitches

Some Terms

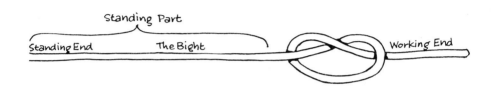

7

The Working End or Running End of a rope is the part used in tying the knot.

The Standing Part is the whole of the rest of the rope, i.e. the part not used in tying the knot.

The Standing End is a short region at the end of the Standing Part.

The Bight is the region extending all the way from the Standing End to the Running End. Thus a knot which is tied 'in the bight' is one which is tied without use of either end.

However, the same word is also used in quite a different sense to mean a loop made without use of the end; we had an example in Chapter 1 when in coiling a rope, *a bight* was thrust through the centre at the finish.

A Knot is anything deliberately tied in rope, twine, etc.

A Bend is a knot for joining two ropes.

A Hitch is a knot for joining a rope to a support.

Open Loop, Closed Loop, and Turn are illustrated in Fig. 8.

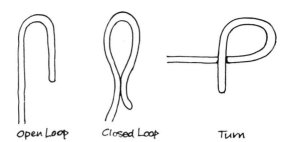

Open Loop   Closed Loop   Turn   **8**

A **Round Turn** is the name applied to two turns; there is seldom any need to use it, still less to refer to three turns as two round turns (Fig. 9).

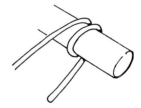

9

A **Single Hitch** is a turn made round a support and arranged as in Fig. 10. It usually forms part of some more complex hitch.

10

A **Half Hitch** is a Single Hitch made round the standing part of some other hitch, as in the Round Turn and Two Half Hitches (see later).

Strength. The strength of a rope is the force in lb, kg, or tons weight required to break it. If a rope makes a sharp turn on entering a knot, only the parts on the outside of the sharply bent portion will be stretched; the break will therefore start here, and spread across the rope. That is the explanation of why a rope often breaks at or near the point of entry. However, even in new ropes plenty of breaks occur far from any knot, and the reason is not well understood. A knot free from any sharp turn near the point of entry is said to have *a good lead*.

Knots are graded in strength according to how much or how little they reduce the strength of a rope. Figures are available, ranging from roughly 10% to 50% reduction. Where there is danger from failure rope should not be used at more than 10% of its rated strength, and the Table on p.13 should clarify the choice. Strength is therefore not the most important feature of a knot. Much confusion is caused by people, particularly mountaineers, who use the word 'strength' to include 'security'.

Security is resistance to becoming untied while in use. A good knot should hold well under strain, and should break readily to be taken apart when required. Security is vitally important; it is affected by the nature of the rope, whether stiff or supple, rough or smooth, thick or thin, and whether the two ropes are of equal or unequal thickness. Very few bends can be relied upon to hold well if there is a large difference in thickness. Bends involving materials other than rope can cause special problems, as is shown by the following extreme case.

The Sheet Bend is well known to be more secure than the Reef, and the Double Sheet Bend considerably more secure. But one day I happened to be looking out of my bedroom window while holding a length of 10mm braid-on-braid polyester, and I noticed that it would not reach the ground. I thought of fire, and tried tying it first with a Sheet Bend and then with a Double Sheet Bend to a band of cotton material, the sash of my dressing gown. In both cases the knot came apart with only a moderate pull! Perversely I tried a Reef, and the bend held firmly! There is no knowing what may happen if unusual materials are used, but do not be misled by this tale into having faith in the Reef. The supreme authority Clifford Ashley (calling it the Square Knot) says of it:

> "There have probably been more lives lost as a result of using a Square Knot as a bend (to join two ropes together) than from the failure of any other half dozen knots combined."

*A Hitch for Thick to Thin

A common requirement is to join a relatively thin heaving line to the much thicker hawser for towing. Not many knots are suitable, but this simple hitch works well. Raise one strand of the hawser, using a marlinspike if necessary; pass the thin line beneath it against the lay, and add an overhand knot as stopper. Then put on two single hitches as shown, and the job is done (Fig. 11).

11

The action of the two single hitches is interesting: each reduces the pull transmitted across it, so that there is little or no strain on the stopper knot, which is unlikely even to be pulled up against the rope, and is almost superfluous. Fig. 11a shows an alternative arrangement.

11a

Sense

Like rope, coils, turns or hitches can be made right-handed or left-handed. Fig. 12 shows a *right-handed coil; the line rotates clockwise away from the observer*, with the arrows. Also, of course, *it rotates anticlockwise towards the observer*, against the arrows.

12

Fig. 13 shows two right-handed turns, and Fig. 13a two left-handed turns.

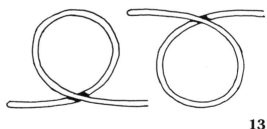

13

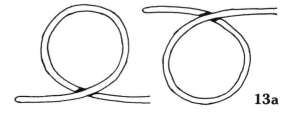

13a

The concept of sense is essential to the system of knotting presented in this book, but even experienced knotters find it hard to grasp. Make one left-handed and one right-handed turn, fix with a spot of glue, and if you like, cut the ends to equal length. Notice that they can be turned over or placed in any position and the sense will remain unaltered. By contrast, if you rotate your hand in a direction which for you is clockwise, a person opposite you will see the motion as anticlockwise; these terms should therefore be avoided whenever possible. **The sense, as described here, is of vital importance in understanding later chapters.**

Control of Sense

With the hands a foot or so apart and palms downwards, hold the rope between thumb and index of each hand. With the right hand rotate the rope clockwise, as when screwing in a screw; this is most conveniently done by *rolling* the rope **away** from the tip of the index finger. At the same time that you roll the rope, bring the two hands together. You will find that the combined actions have produced a left-handed turn. Roll the other way, **towards** the index tip, to get a right-handed turn. Having got the sense right, the position in space may readily be adjusted to bring the loop above, below, or to one side or the other of the straight portion. In copying a knot from this or any other book it is often convenient first to note the sense of a turn, then to copy it by 'rolling' the rope, and finally to adjust the position to match the illustration.

On a sleepless night, with the eyes closed but the mind's eye wide open, make right-handed and left-handed hitches or turns in various positions and note whether the running or standing end passes behind or in front of the part it crosses. It is better than counting sheep!

Hitches with Two Turns

The Clove Hitch

This famous hitch consists simply of two single hitches, both of the same sense. It can be tied in three ways.

Method (i) (Fig. 14)
To put the hitch on to a ring or any structure where there is no free end, the clove must be worked with one end of the rope. To get both hitches of the same sense, take the end over (or under) the ring the first time, then the same way the second time.

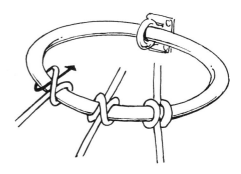

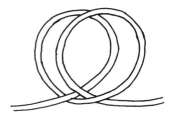

Method (ii) (Fig. 15)   **14**
First 'roll' a single hitch (say) left-handed, by moving the right thumb away from the index tip; then roll a second one of the same sense to the right of it. Slide the right one over the left, and drop the pair over the end of the support.

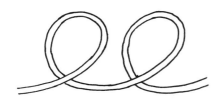

15

Method (iii)

Before tying the hitch, carry out the following exercise. Form the two single hitches side-by-side as in Method (ii) above. Bring the fingers of the left and right hands towards you through the left and right loops from the far side (Fig. 15a). Now, without changing the grip of the two hands, rotate the wrists to make the rope straighten out into a length running away from you. That completes the exercise, but don't let go!

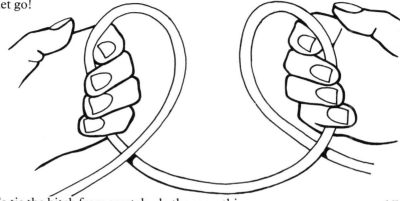

15a

To tie the hitch from scratch, do the same thing backwards: seize a straight piece of rope by the grip present at the end of the exercise; then *reverse the twist of the wrists*, and in so doing create the two previous hitches simultaneously; almost in the same motion slide the one over the other to complete the Clove Hitch dramatically in no time at all.

The Clove Hitch is often recommended as a mooring hitch, but it should be remembered that it is not secure against a snatching pull, particularly if the direction is variable. However, it has the advantage that after sufficient practice it can be tied with one hand without great difficulty. For example, you may have rowed out to your boat in the dinghy, and are standing in it holding on to the guard rail with one hand while with the other you tie the painter to a stanchion with a Clove Hitch. It will hold while you climb on board, after which you can apply something more substantial. As with any hitch, a Clove may be made more secure either by adding a stopper knot or by finishing with one or two half hitches round the standing part. You can, of course, take both measures.

Slipped Hitches

For quick release, any hitch may be served up in slipped form by taking a bight instead of the end through as the last tuck. Fig. 16 shows a Round Turn (two single turns) and a single slipped Half Hitch round the mast for use when being towed. The knot would slip extremely easily, and would need careful watching. If you need to move aft to take the tiller, substitute a Halter Hitch (page 31), which, however, might require a sharp pull to release it.

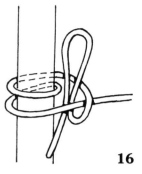

16

The Cow Hitch or Lark's Head

The knot is made up of two single hitches of opposite sense. To tie it, turn back a short length at the end of the rope (Fig. 17), then fold the closed end over to make two loops (Fig. 18), and slip both onto the post (Fig. 19). If the end of the post is not free, the hitch must be worked with the end of the rope, which takes longer. Though it looks good, it is probably the least secure of all hitches. Put one round any smooth rod, work the standing part back and forth a few times, and the hitch will come off. (The idea that it is used to tether cows in the open is utterly nonsensical. I have enquired in Guernsey, which is one of the few places where cows are tethered in the open, and find that a halter – of which there are several designs – is fitted to the head and joined by a rope to a metal swivel on the end of a metal rod driven into the ground. No cow hitch is involved.)

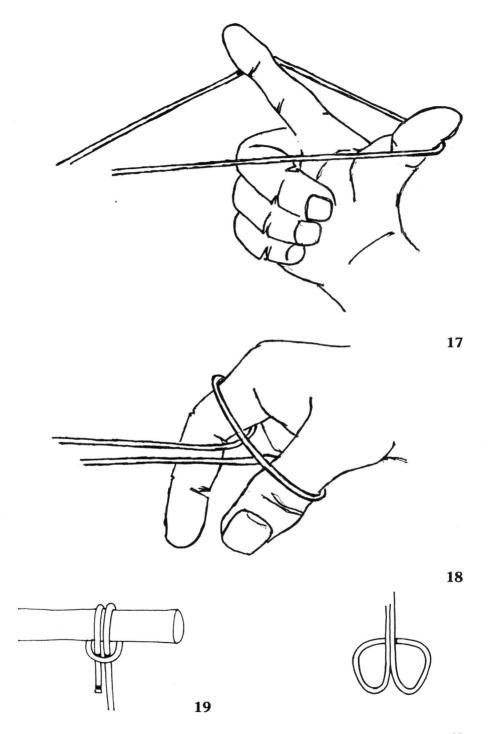

17

18

19

The Cow Hitch is perfectly safe if the strain is on both ends, whether held together or separately. It is used with two long ends to put through the clew of a small sail when each end forms one of the two sheets used to trim the sail (Fig. 20). An Overhand Knot serves equally well (Fig. 21).

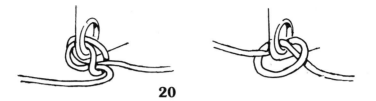

20   **21**

*The Pedigree Cow

One extra tuck transforms this least secure of all hitches into one of the most secure. The hitch with the last tuck put through the opposite way has long been known; I have tucked it the way shown to allow me to award it the title it deserves (Fig. 22).

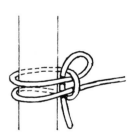

22

The Fisherman's Bend or Anchor Bend

This so-called bend is really a hitch. Make two single turns round the post, then tuck the working end under both turns (Fig. 23). The hitch is extremely secure, and is ideal for mooring a boat to a post.

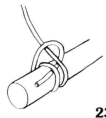

23

Knots under water come undone in an inexplicable way, so to join to an anchor it is wise to add a stopper knot, or two half hitches round the standing part.

Round Turn and Two Half Hitches

First wind on two turns, then add the two half hitches round the standing part of the rope, the second farther from the spar than the first. With a horizontal bar, if you take the rope *over* the bar with the two turns, then you take it *over* the rope with both half hitches (Figs 24 and 25).

This hitch is widely used because not only is it a firm attachment to start with, but the second end of the rope can be fixed with a second round turn and two half hitches, put on against a strong pull from the load while the whole thing stays tight. If you are tying, say, a rolled-up mattress to the roof rack of a car, start with a round turn and two half hitches on one side of the rack, take the rope round the load, then pull tight and maintain the tension as you take the rope twice (or if needs be, three times) round the bar on the opposite side before adding the final two half hitches.

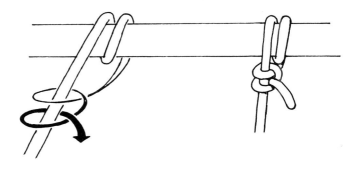

24   25

Pile Hitch

This elegant but practical hitch is not as well known as it should be. Make a bight in the rope, not necessarily at one end; with one hand make a turn round the post with the doubled part, winding *upwards* and keeping the closed end of the bight at the bottom; then drop the loop over the post with the other hand (Fig. 26). All done in no time, and ideal for mooring. (See also: Double Pile Hitch, p.34.)

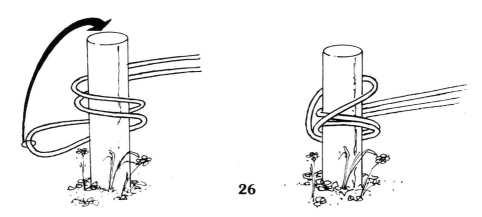

26

Hitches with One Turn

Figure-of-Eight Hitch

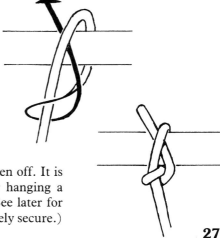

This hitch is quickly tied and easily taken off. It is not very secure, but is convenient for hanging a selection of different ropes on a rail. (See later for Figure-of-Eight Noose, which is extremely secure.)

27

Halter Hitch

Though it gets its name from its use in tethering a horse, it is a good general purpose quick-release hitch. It consists simply of a noose made with a slipped overhand knot (Fig. 28).

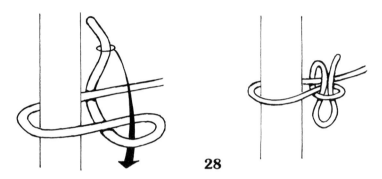

28

Marlinspike (Marlinespike, Marlingspike) Hitch

This hitch allows the pull on a fine line to be made with a marlinspike to prevent the line biting into the hand, as when pulling on a tight whipping. With the standing part attached to the load make a slipped overhand knot by slipping a bight of the *standing part* through the loop, and push the marlinspike into this bight (Fig. 29).

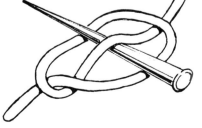

29

A professional will use the following method: With the standing end already attached to the load make a loose turn (hitch) round the marlinspike (or round whatever you are using instead). When you have done this a good many times you will probably find that without realizing it you have gradually progressed to getting the same result by moving the tip of the marlinspike in a circle and doing very little with the other hand. Then, somewhat as a crochet worker picks up a thread, with the marlinspike you pick up a bight of the standing part and pull it through the hitch; and there is your marlinspike hitch already in place on the marlinspike.

Timber Hitch

The only drawback to this brilliant hitch is that it can easily be tied incorrectly by beginners. In Figure 30, note that the working end is twisted round its own part, **not** round the standing part; three times round is usually plenty. It is quickly put on, supremely secure, and never jams. Because there is only one turn round the support, not much rope is used, and the hitch is well suited for use round (say) a thick tree trunk, though with wide objects more twists may be needed.

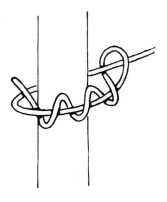

30

The Problem of Longitudinal Pull

The hitches described so far have all been for withstanding a pull transverse to a spar; none of them can be relied upon to withstand a pull along it.

Killick Hitch

To drag a spar or tree trunk it is evidently best to have the hitch at the far end. However, if you put a Timber Hitch there the trunk is bound to swing round to bring the hitch to your end. The ingenious remedy is to add a single hitch at the near end (Fig. 31).

31

Rolling Hitch

This famous hitch is made with a thin line put round a relatively much thicker rope to exert a pull along it. It is a Clove Hitch with the first turn repeated. Before the thin line will grip it must be tightened by a pull on both the running end and the standing part; it will then hold well as long as the tension is maintained (Fig. 32). It can be used to enable several hands to haul on the same relatively thin rope to free a thicker one jammed in a winch, or take the thin line to a second winch.

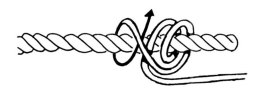

32

An odd feature is that if a hand is placed over the knot itself, it can be made to slide along the thick rope and off the end, when it will pull out into a straight piece. As we shall see, this means that the hitch can be tied in the bight, though there is no advantage in doing so. The hitch will always hold well between one rope and another thicker one, and it will usually hold on a spar, though it cannot be relied on completely to do so.

Double Pile Hitch

This hitch is swiftly tied by repeating the first turn of a Pile Hitch; it is a recent invention by my friend John Smith, and is even more effective than a Rolling Hitch for effecting a longitudinal pull on a smooth spar (Fig. 33). A third turn is unlikely ever to be required.

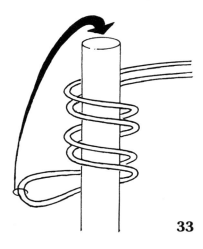

33

*Clara Hitch

To join a thin rope to the end of a much thicker one, make two turns with the standing part of the thin rope (Fig. 34) but finish with the working end as shown (Figs 34a&b). If the hitch is to be made on to the middle of the thick rope, tie the whole of the hitch with the working end. It can be quickly tied, and holds well on rope, but with two turns only is useless on a spar. However, the grip produced

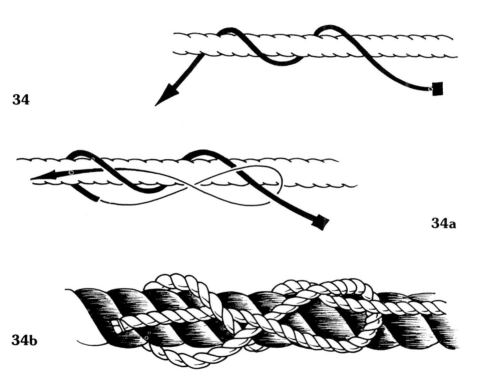

34

34a

34b

increases dramatically with more turns, and four turns are sufficient even for a smooth spar, but you can add an extra one or two for a margin of safety.

If ever you need to pull fairly hard on a thin line for long enough to be uncomfortable, a Clara Hitch on to a short length of thicker rope can provide relief.

Hitches Used as Binding Knots

The Strangle Knot

Start as if to tie an Overhand Knot, but instead of making the tuck, go round the spar a second time, before tucking the end through both turns (Fig. 35). It is a double overhand knot, and just like the Constrictor (see below) it binds tightly and is hard to remove (Fig. 36). Tied in an end it makes a firm, attractive stopper knot.

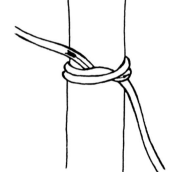

35   **36**

Constrictor Hitch

To tie with an end, first make a Clove Hitch, and then add the extra tuck as shown (Fig. 37). To tie it in the bight (Fig. 38): make a right-handed loop hanging down (Fig. 39), insert your left index finger through the part shown, and, while keeping it straight, rotate the tip in one complete circle, as shown (Fig. 40). You now have a constrictor hitch on your finger waiting to be slipped off onto where it is needed (Fig. 41).

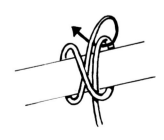

37

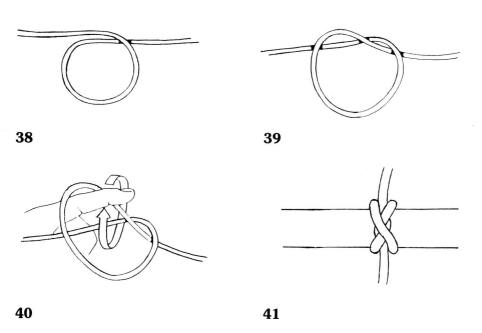

38

39

40

41

The knot binds so tightly that it is hard to take off, and the rope may have to be cut. Note that it consists of an overhand knot covered by a diagonal strand which holds it down in the manner of a 'finger on', an action which accounts for its peculiar properties.

It is convenient for use as a temporary whipping swiftly applied, or for closing a sack or bag (e.g. a bouquet garni). If the sack is to be opened, make the last tuck with a bight to produce a slipped version.

Marlinspike Constrictor Hitch

To follow the present enthusiasm for use of the Constrictor, simply use a marlinspike in place of the finger.

Hitches for a Long Bundle

Marline Hitch and Half Hitch

A Marline Hitch is an Overhand Knot in disguise (Fig. 42). A series of them may be used to secure any long bundle, or, for example, to lash a furled sail to its spar. They are more secure than half hitches (Fig. 43), but more laborious to put on because a long end must be pulled through each time. (They look deceptively like Half Hitches. Get a friend to tie some of each, and learn to distinguish them.)

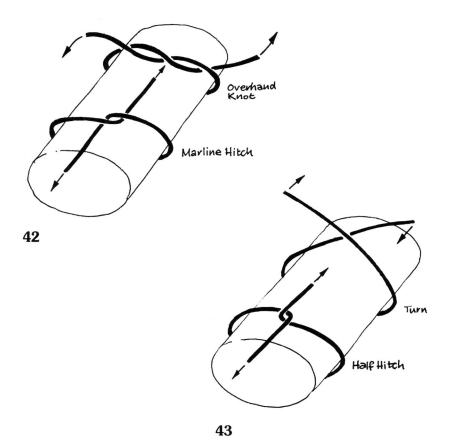

Overhand
Knot

Marline Hitch

42

Turn

Half Hitch

43

Chain Stitch Lashing

This hitch provides a quick way of securing a long untidy bundle or fastening down a furled sail temporarily for quick release. Start with a Timber Hitch, then put on chain stitches by passing each of a series of bights alternatively over and under the spar and through the previous bight. Take the end through the last bight, then finish with a Clove round the spar, as shown (Fig. 44), or belay to a cleat.

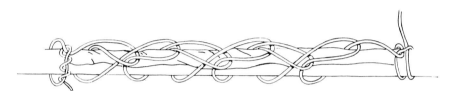

44

Do and Undo

Both the Pile Hitch and the Constrictor were described as being tied 'in the bight' and slipped over the end of the support; but this method cannot be used when the support has no end (e.g. as on a ring). To learn to tie with an end, first make a 'model' hitch in the bight, and put it over any convenient support with a free end. Then *undo* the last tuck, and watch carefully what you do as you put it back. Next remove two tucks, and retie them, and continue until you have undone the whole hitch and have retied it by use of the end. Some knots, such as the Pile Hitch, may be tedious to learn in this way, but the method is infallible.

The principle has a broader application, and may be applied to any knot however tied. To invent a new method of tying an old knot, simply try various methods of *untying* it, and reverse them.

*The Law of Loop, Hitch and Bight

The Law follows the principle of 'Do and Undo'. Suppose you know how to tie a certain hitch with an end, but you would like to find out if it can be tied in the bight. Simply slip the hitch off its support and pull the two ends apart. If it pulls out straight, i.e. if it unties in the bight, it follows that it must be possible to tie it in the bight. It may, however, require a great deal of practice.

In the case of Loops (Chapter 6), if a loop can be undone without use of the ends, evidently it can be tied in the bight. Once more, different methods of tying will be revealed by the various possible ways of untying it.

3 Traditional Bends

A bend is a knot for joining two ropes, and in this book there are two kinds:

(i) **Traditional Bends.** These are good sound knots, tested through the ages, and yet invented how, why or when – we seldom know.

(ii) **Knots which fit into the new scientific system presented in this book for the first time.** They are given in Chapters 4 and 5.

The two categories overlap because the new system, which generates only symmetrical knots, also produces most of that small proportion of traditional knots which are symmetrical too.

Most of the drawings show one light and one dark rope and it will help if you can use corresponding coloured ropes for the work. (Addresses on page 88 show where such rope can be obtained by post; alternatively it is a simple matter to colour a few inches of a white rope with Indian ink.)

How to Understand the Instructions

It is assumed that the book is laid flat on the table, and therefore 'up' and 'down' mean 'up *out of* the page' (towards your face) or 'down *into* it' (away from your face); they do *not* refer to directions towards the top or bottom of the page. Directions on the page itself are shown by N, S, E or W, as on a map.

Overhand Knot and Half Knot

Both have the same structure, but:

The Overhand Knot (or Thumb Knot) is tied in a single length of rope, often with use of one end only, as when tying a stopper knot (Fig. 45).

The Half Knot is tied with two ends, as in the first stage of tying the shoelaces or a reef knot (Fig. 46).

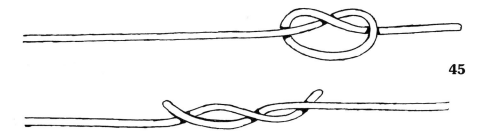

45

46

The Whatnot

We will start with an odd one, with no guarantee attached. At the start the two ropes run East and West, the dark lying to the North of the light one, with a gap between them (Fig. 47). Take the *dark end South* over the light rope, and the *light end North* over the dark one (Fig. 48); then bring *both ends up through the gap* (Fig. 49).

Pull strongly, and note that the bend holds well (Fig. 50). To undo, hold the knot itself and grasp the two ends between finger and thumb at the root, and twist so that they first uncross and then cross again in the reverse direction (Fig. 51). Now pull gently on the two standing parts, and the bend will fall apart. This dramatic instability has kept the bend out of general use, though it could be argued that the ease of undoing is a valuable feature. The reader must form his own opinion.

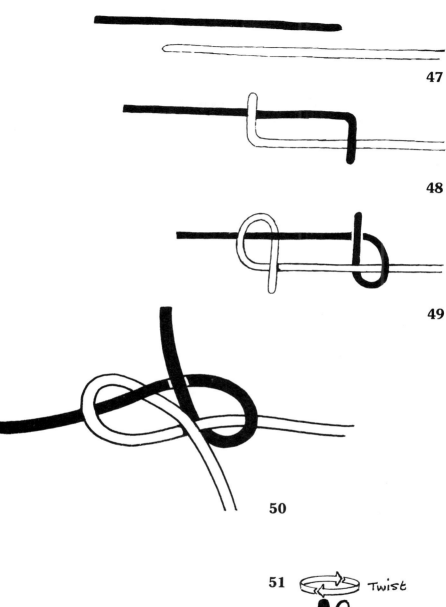

47

48

49

50

51 Twist

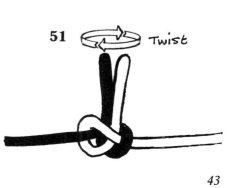

The Double Harness Bend

The start is as for the Whatnot (Figs. 52 & 53), but this time, after each end has crossed over the other rope it is taken back, right across the under-side of the gap (Fig. 54), before turning upwards outside it, and then down through it (Fig. 55). To break, force apart the two half hitches. The knot is neat (Fig. 56), secure and not hard to break; a good general purpose bend.

It has been well known for a long time. However, surprisingly, in his book, *The Complete Rigger: Wire and Rope* (1985), Brion Toss describes it with lavish praise as an invention by Mr John "Fud" Benson, made around 1983, and names it accordingly 'The Benson Bend'.

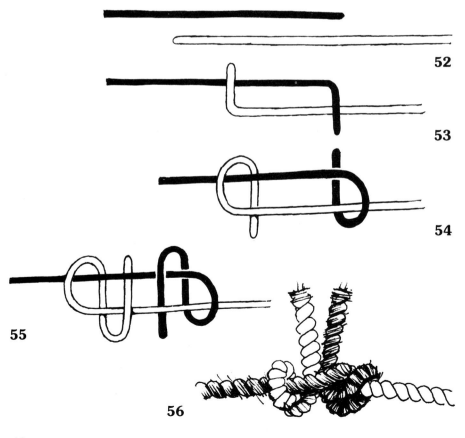

52

53

54

55

56

The Fisherman's Knot, Englishman's Knot, or Water Knot

Start with the now familiar setting: Dark north, Light south (Fig. 57), and crossing as before with a gap between them (Fig. 58). Take both ends all the way across the gap on the under-side, but finish by taking each down through its own half hitch to complete an overhand knot on each side (Fig. 59). The two then slide together and lock to form a secure bend (Fig. 60). If the knot has not jammed hard, the two can be made to slide apart with a pull on each end.

(To prepare the mind for the next chapter, note that both half hitches are of the same sense, in this case right-handed. As an exercise you can try tying a left-handed version, or a mixed version with one half right-handed and the other left-handed.)

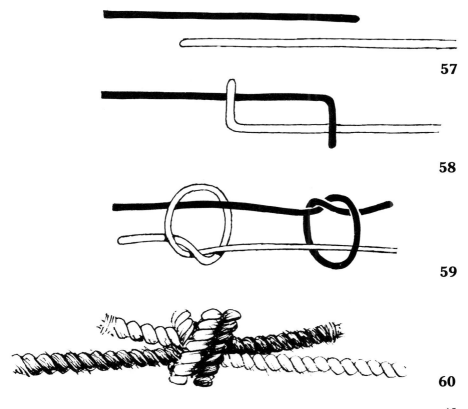

57

58

59

60

Sliding Figure-of-Eight Knot

Similar start (Figs. 61 & 62). Dark goes: up through the gap, up through it again, then down through the first half hitch. Light does the same (Figs. 63, 64 & 65). *Concentrate*: this knot can be madly confusing when it goes wrong.

It is a better knot than the last one (The Fisherman's); even more secure, less prone to jam, and well worth the effort of learning it.

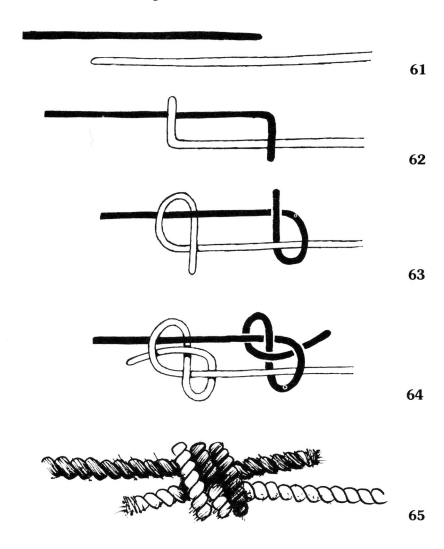

61

62

63

64

65

Reef Knot

Make a Half Knot, starting 'left over right' (Fig. 66); then add the second Half Knot 'right over left' (Fig. 67). To confirm, check that, on each side the two ends pass either both above or both below the part that crosses them (Fig. 68).

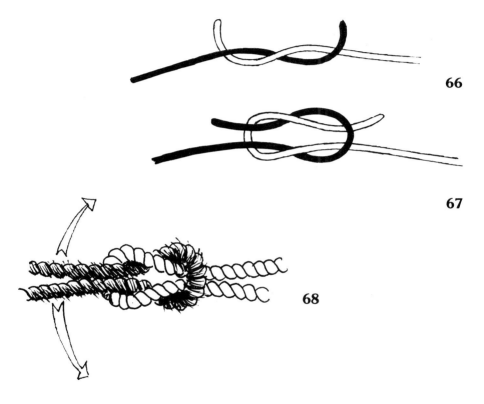

66

67

68

A reef can usually be broken by a sharp pull to separate the two parts of one rope (Figs. 68 & 69). The Cow Hitch so formed can then slide off its straight partner.

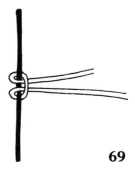

69

The popular but erroneous belief that the Reef is a safe bend has led to many deaths. It is extremely unsafe with ropes of different thicknesses, and not entirely safe even with identical ropes, although it appears to be so. To escape from a fire, yes, you can tie a reef in two sheets, but only if you tie a stopper knot in each one before tying the reef, and it needs practice. Happy landings!

The common and correct use of the reef is to join the two ends of a rope, as when reefing a sail, finishing a parcel, or tying up a plant. For example, to tie up a sunflower, slip a Constrictor Hitch over the supporting stick, then draw up the first Half Knot to bring the loop round the stem to a size that will allow room for growth, then fix that size with the second Half Knot. There are very few bends that can be used in this way, and life would be difficult without the Reef.

Reef and Granny Bows

The slipped form of any knot is made by making the last tuck with a bight instead of with the end. For a Reef Bow, tuck bights of both ends.

The Granny is not a knot, it is a mistake made by tying 'right over left' (Fig. 70) and then 'right over left' again for the second half. It either slips or jams. The Granny Bow on a shoe proclaims the ignorance of its owner even at a distance by the way it lies along the shoe instead of neatly across it as in a Reef Bow (Fig. 71). However, because it is not under tension – dare we say it – it can hold as well as a Reef Bow.

70

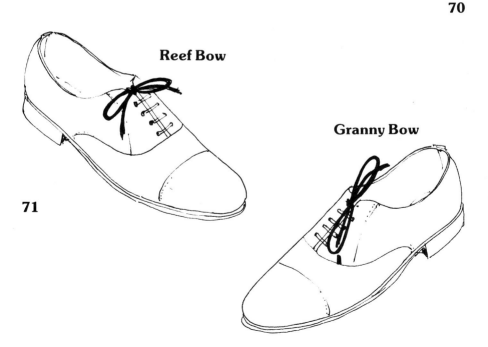

Reef Bow

Granny Bow

71

The Sheet Bend

Introductory Exercise

With the dark rope make a Half Hitch, as illustrated; then bring the light end up through it. Grasp the two parts firmly together with thumb on top and index below (Fig. 72).

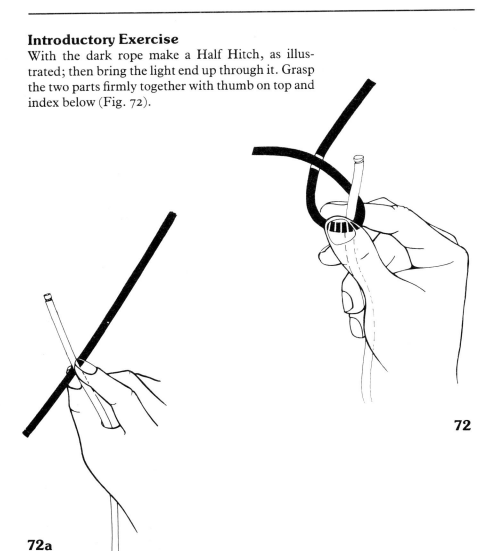

72

72a

Next, *undo* what has been done by 'unwinding' the Half Hitch with the left hand while at the same time making an unscrewing action with the right wrist. You should now be left with a straight piece of light rope crossing over a straight piece of dark rope (Fig. 72a).

To Tie the Knot

Start where you ended the exercise with two crossed straight pieces. Now reverse the action performed in the exercise, thus achieving in one smooth swift action the half-way stage of tying the knot as shown in Fig. 72, which was the start of the introductory exercise. Finish by taking the light end behind the dark standing part and down through the Half Hitch, as shown (Figs. 73 & 74).

73

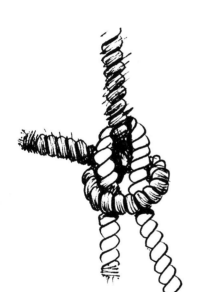

74

The Sheet Bend is neat, and very quick to tie; it is perhaps more widely used than any other bend, but even so it is not completely dependable and should not be used in any perilous circumstance, especially if the rope is synthetic. With ropes differing widely in thickness the bend is unsound. When the difference is small enough to be tolerated, the open loop (the 'hook') should be made with the thicker rope, and the half hitch with the thinner one.

The Double Sheet Bend

This bend is thoroughly sound. The only difference from the previous knot is that two turns instead of one are made with the dark rope at the start (Fig. 75); the completion is the same. It takes no more than a split second to make the extra turn, and the Double Sheet Bend is the form to use (Fig. 76).

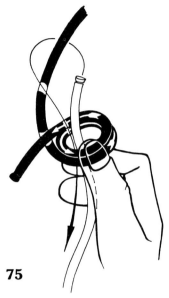

75

76

The Becket Hitch

This is best thought of as a *bend* in which the 'hook' of the Single or Double Sheet Bend is replaced by a loop, which may be either tied or spliced. A hawser for towing will have a permanent loop spliced at one end (Fig. 77).

77

4 Introducing the New System

Before starting on the system itself, three precursors will be introduced. They came at the stage when I had decided that the way to try for new bends was to think of the two halves separately, and then decide how to put them together. There seemed to be no better way than to start with the two halves that make up the famous Sheet Bend, i.e. an open loop and a single hitch.

*Simple Simon Over

Tie as shown (Fig. 78), and note that, as in the Sheet Bend, the two running ends should emerge on the same side of the knot (Fig. 79). Taking the running end round a second time produces a Double Simon Over (Fig. 80).

78

79

80

*Simple Simon Under

This second version takes slightly longer to tie. At the intersection, the light end passes beneath the standing part; the nip thereby imparted to it considerably increases security, and the bend is effective with quite large differences in thickness of the two ropes (Fig. 81).

81

*Vice Versa

Start as for a Single Sheet Bend (Fig. 82), but then make a complete turn round the dark standing part before taking the end out through the dark half hitch. Finish by taking the dark end through the light loop (Fig. 83). The bend is symmetrical and decorative (Fig. 84). Figs 83 and 84 show opposite faces.

82

83

84

The System

The next step was made on what was, for me, a momentous occasion: the Inaugural Meeting of the International Guild of Knot Tyers on Saturday, 17 April 1982, held aboard the Maritime Trust's vessel R.R.S. *Discovery*, berthed in St Katharine's Dock in the lee of Tower Bridge, London. On that day I learned two principles I might never have found from any amount of reading. They were:

(1) That every knot can be tied in either right-handed or left-handed form.

(2) That if a knot is symmetrical, it is likely to be a good one. A mathematician went further and said: "If it's not symmetrical, I throw it away!"

Rigger's Bend

This bend was dramatically introduced to the British public in an eleven-inch front-page column of *The Times* of 6 October 1978, where it was attributed to Dr Hunter, who was unaware that it had already been described in about 1950 in *Knots for Mountaineers* by Phil. D. Smith, an American, who named it simply: 'A Rigger's Bend'. It is a good general purpose bend which will serve well here as an example of an established knot which is symmetrical, and which can be tied according to the rules of the system.

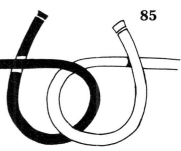

85

RR, Up-Opp

In Fig. 85 note that the dark loop on the left is right-handed: the end screws clockwise down into the paper as it recedes from the observer. If there is any confusion on this critically important point, return to p.22 for revision. The light loop is also right-handed, unscrewing up towards the observer out of the paper. All knots in the system are described by a code; at this stage the code is **RR**, **indicating that both turns are right-handed.**

Next note that the two loops are combined by the light end being brought *up* through the dark loop. **The dark end lies at the bottom of** the assembly and the **light end at the top**; thus **the two ends are said to be Opposed.**

Up to this stage the code is: **RR, Up-Opp**. The word '**up**' (or in other cases 'down') always refers to the initial move of the *Light End*.

The position now reached is known as the Starting Position, or *START* (Fig. 85). To finish the bend, take the *Light End UP* and the *Dark End DOWN* through the common centre, as shown (Fig. 86), without crossing either over the other. The complete code is: **Rigger . . . RR, Up-Opp; U & D Centre, Don't Cross.** Now tighten up (Fig. 87). The bend is secure, quickly tied, and not hard to break if you start by pushing apart the two 'collars' indicated (Fig. 88). The method is general: to break any knot, start by looking for one or more 'collars' (I thank my friend John Smith for the word).

RR, Up-Opp; U&D Centre

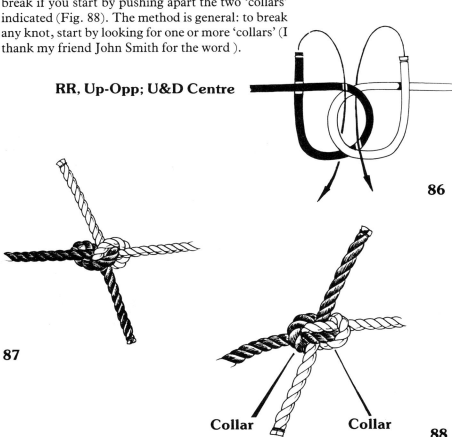

86

87

Collar　　　**Collar**

88

The Alpine Butterfly Bend

This knot has been much used by mountaineers in the form of a loop since ancient times, but it was not until 1975 that Brion Toss, a well known figure in the knotting world had the idea of tying it as a bend. Elated thereby, he named it *'The Strait Bend'*, and wrote: "My own contribution to the world of knots is this one, named after the strait of Juan de Fuca in the Pacific Northwest." However, because it is now known that *any* loop knot can be transformed into the corresponding bend I think it is best to call both forms by the same name.

To tie the bend by the system, the **START** is: **RL, Up-Same** (Fig. 89).

The **RL** indicates that the **dark loop is right-handed** and the **light loop is left-handed.**

Up indicates that the light end comes **up through the dark loop.**

Same shows that both ends finish on the **same side** (beneath the loops).

The code for the finished knot is: **Alpine Butterfly Bend: RL, Up-Same; Down Centre.**

Down Centre: both ends go down the common centre (Fig. 89a).

The bend is neat, secure and easy to break; everything you want, but not yet widely known. (Fig. 90)

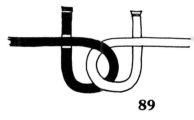

89

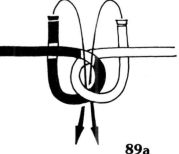

89a

90

Abbreviated Codes

One of the useful features claimed for the system is that it enables a knot to be described by one knotter to another without the need for an illustration. Another is that a knot is easier to remember in coded form than as a vision in the mind's eye or a vague recall of finger movements. But the code for the Rigger **RR, Up-Opp; U & D Centre, Don't Cross** is lengthy, and the reader will do well, after some experience, to produce his own private shortened form.

One approach is to remember that Sherlock Holmes was alerted by the dog *not* barking in the night. Omission can be informative. So in general, if the Light Loop is left-handed, write **RL**; if it is right-handed, omit both letters to indicate **RR**. Similarly, if there is no crossing, omit that section.

All that remains now is: **Up-Opp; U & D Centre**. As it happens, **U & D** is always followed by the word 'Centre', so that word can go out too. For me now the code for the Rigger is: **UP-Opp; U & D**. Not hard to remember! But there can be difficulties if you try to inflict your personal code on someone else.

Shake Hands

The code is: **RR, Down-Opp; U & D Centre, Cross South**. The Figure explains the important new method of crossing (Figs. 91 & 92) where the dark end passes South (or South-east) over the light end. It is important to remember that the crossing instruction is always for the dark end to cross *over* the light end.

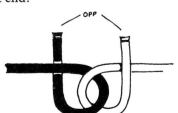

91

CROSS SOUTH

92

Though this knot is new as a bend, Ashley (1944) gives two methods of tying the corresponding loop (Nos. 1031, 1048). It is hard to understand why this excellent knot, whether loop or bend, has passed almost unnoticed, when in fact it is one of the very best, being not only secure, but easily broken, neat in appearance with the ends parallel to the leads, and simple to tie (Fig. 93). Perhaps the neglect was Ashley's fault, for he describes the loop as decorative and suitable for a handbag handle, whereas in fact both bend and loop are well suited to most applications, and it is hard to find a better bend or a better loop. For the method of deriving a loop from a bend, see p.81.

*Eastern Zeppelin

Code: **RL, Light over Dark; U & D Centre, Cross East.** The left-handed light loop is simply laid on top of the dark one (Fig. 94); the illustration shows the only way this can be done symmetrically. (For example, if you try this with the light end pointing North, you find that this end lies sandwiched in the middle of the knot, and the dark end is at the bottom.) Finally the light end is brought up through the centre, and the dark end crosses Eastward *over* it.

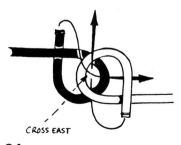

CROSS EAST

94

95

The original Zeppelin Knot, or Rosendahl Bend, was named after Charles Rosendahl who ordered the airship he commanded to be tethered with it because no other bend was as secure or easy to break. In the original version the final tuck was made without crossing; but 'Cross East' brings the ends out perpendicular to the leads (Fig. 95), so I prefer it, but only for looks; the performance is the same. The bend shows the odd but useful feature that even if it works loose in response to a snatching pull, it will tighten again each time the tug is renewed. Practically nothing is known about why one bend will hold well and another will not, and if ever the problem is worked out perhaps it will be by someone brooding over a Zeppelin Knot.

5 More on the New System

Wider fields now open up as we move on, first to make tucks through regions other than the centre, and then to discover new Starting Positions.

The Carrick Bend

For a knotter to go out into the world not knowing the traditional method of tying a Carrick Bend would be like not recognizing the national anthem, so it is given here. For two ways to tie it according to the system, see later in this chapter under the headings 'Corrick' and 'Carrick's Cousin'.

Carrick by Traditional Method

Look first at Fig. 98 showing the completed bend in its 'flat' form. Notice that by itself, each half is nothing but a half hitch, and that the two are interlinked by each rope passing alternately over and under some part the whole way round. To tie it, with the dark rope make a right-handed turn with the end directed towards you (Fig. 96); then with the light rope start 'over-over', and continue 'under-over-under-over-under' to complete the knot (Figs. 97 & 98). Pull on the two standing parts, and the knot capsizes dramatically into the completely different final and stable form (Fig. 98a).

96

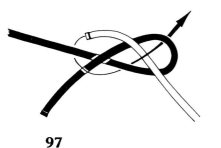

97

98

The Carrick is a bend of great importance, and
was the one most used aboard the old sailing ships.
The prominent features are the ease with which it
can be broken, and its noble symmetry. For use with
hawsers it is usually left in the flat form with the ends
seized to the standing parts.

98a

The Corrick

This interesting bend first appeared unnamed in the
Ashley Book of Knots (1944). I have taken the liberty
of naming it 'The Corrick' to show its relation to the
Carrick. The code is: **Corrick: RR, Down-Same;
Light North and Down Dark Loop; Dark South
and Down Light Loop.**

Notice that because the start is **'Same'**, the two
final tucks are made in the *same* direction (both
down). Tie from the code and the Figure (Fig. 99).

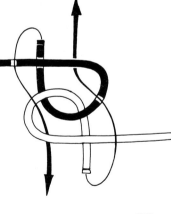

99

100

The Corrick is a neat bend, resembling the Carrick in both performance and structure (Fig. 100), but unlike the Carrick it makes a simple and effective loop (see Chapter 6, p.81). The relationship to the Carrick is well shown by the code for tying the Carrick from the same starting position (Fig. 101). **Carrick: RR, Down-Same: Light North and Up Dark Loop; Dark South and Up Light Loop.**

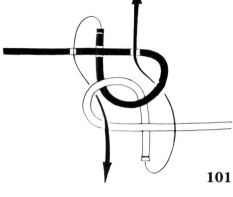

101

*Carrick's Cousin

Here we introduce a new Starting Position: **RR, Down Middle**. To make it, take the light end South below the dark loop, then complete as shown (Fig. 102). The meaning of the term 'Down-Middle' is that the light end goes *down*, and the two ends are situated half-way between the top and bottom of the assembly, i.e. in the *middle*. The full code is: **Carrick's Cousin: RR, Down Middle: Cross Dark over Light; Dark up Dark Loop; Light down Light Loop** (Fig. 103).

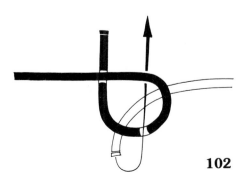

102

Pull up (Fig. 104), and you get a bend which is even easier to break than a Carrick.

103

104

The relationship to the true Carrick is well shown by the code for tying a Carrick from the same starting position (Fig. 105). **Carrick: RR, Down-Middle; Light Up Dark Loop; Dark Down Light Loop.**

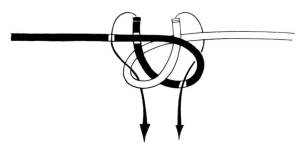

105

The Carrick, the Corrick, and Carrick's Cousin thus form an interesting trio, with Carrick's Cousin the easiest of the three to break.

*Sleeping Beauty

The Starting Position is a new one: **RR, Up-Opp Type 2**. To tie it, take the light end South over the whole of the dark loop, and then up through it. Arrange things so that two 'southern spaces' are formed (see Fig. 105a). To tie the bend, take the light end down, then South, and up the dark southern space. Take the dark end up, then South, and down through the light southern space. Pull up with both leads and both ends to produce an attractive bend which is secure and not hard to break (Fig. 105b). A pull on the two ends helps to loosen it. **Sleeping Beauty: RR, Up-Opp Type 2. Loops.**

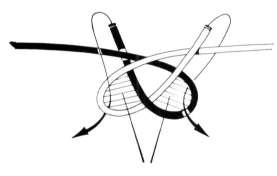

105a   **Southern Spaces**

105b

The code is certainly brief, but a code is meant to be nothing more than a jog to the memory. After a few times you will find yourself making the two tucks through the southern spaces simultaneously, and will get the feel of 'loops' in your fingers.

*The Breakwell Tart

The starting position is basically the same as for
Sleeping Beauty, but this time it is arranged to
produce 'Northern Loops' (see Fig. 105c). The code
for the bend is: **Breakwell: RR, Up-Opp Type 2;
Northern Loops.**

Northern Loops

105c

To make the northern loops, follow the illustration carefully. To tie the bend take the light end
down, then West, and bring it up through the light
northern loop only. Take the dark end down
through the dark northern loop along the path
shown (Fig. 106).

106

The method above follows the way the bend
was revealed by the system. Once tied it can be seen
that it consists of two interlinked Overhand Knots,
and it is probably easier to tie it accordingly. Make a
dark Overhand Knot, and then thread a light Overhand Knot through it, as shown (Fig. 107).

107

Even if pulled up really tight (but by the leads only), like Carrick's Cousin, the bend breaks remarkably easily. It would not be the bend for joining two lengths of thick stiff rope to withstand a snatching pull, but would be well suited for two lengths of soft line under a prolonged steady tension.

108

Breakwell Tart completed (Fig. 108).

6 Loops

The Overhand Loop Knot

This is the loop tied by the ordinary citizen almost by instinct (Fig. 109). It jams, but is useful in string when there is no need to untie it.

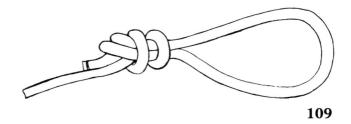

109

Loops from Overhand Knot + Stopper

Fig. 110 illustrates the three spaces within an overhand knot: 's' the standing space; 'c' the central space; and 'r' the running space. In the **Department Store Loop** the stopper returns *up* through the 'c' space (Fig. 111); in the **Honda** (Fig. 112) which is the small fixed loop used in making a lassoo or lariat the stopper passes *down* through the 'r' space, and in the **Farmer's Halter Loop** the stopper passes *down* through the 'c' space (Fig. 113); a fourth but unnamed loop (not illustrated) is made by taking the stoppered end *down* through the 's' space.

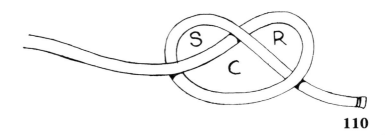

110

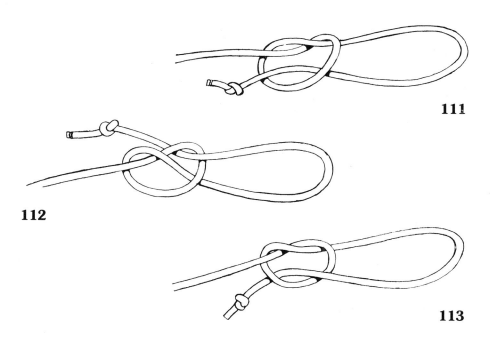

111

112

113

Slipped Overhand Knot + Half Hitch

Tie a slipped Overhand Knot and add a Half Hitch
as shown (Fig. 114). It is a useful loop, quickly tied,
and easily adjustable in length. If the Half Hitch
itself is also slipped (Fig. 115), the whole knot pulls
out into a straight piece if the two ends are pulled.
This result could be foreseen from the way the whole
knot is tied in the bight.

114

115

Improved Englishman's Loop

This loop has the same structure as the Fisherman's Bend of Chapter 3. It is made by tying an Overhand Knot instead of the final Half Hitch in the previous knot (Fig. 116).

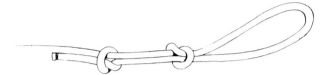

116

The Bowline

The structure of the knot of this loop is the same as that of the Sheet Bend of Chapter 3, Fig. 72, and it is tied in the same way. To make the two descriptions tally, the loop has been drawn as made up of light and dark halves. With thumb and index, index uppermost, press the light end down over the dark standing part (Fig. 117); now repeat precisely the same motions as for tying the Sheet Bend, and the result will be a Bowline (Fig. 118).

117

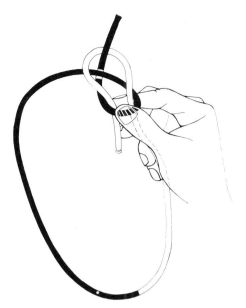

118

Anybody who has learnt only the method given above for tying a bowline can be sadly embarrassed if he tries to tie the loop round a support which he is facing. It is then best to use the following method often taught to children (Fig. 119): first make the half hitch, the rabbit's burrow. The rabbit comes up out of the hole, runs round the tree, and then dives back down the hole (Fig. 120).

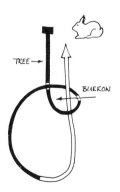

119   **120**

This loop is much used at sea, and has a strange glamour attached to it. The poet and humorist A. P. Herbert was moved to write a poem whose first verse ran:

> "The Bowline is the King of Knots, or
>   if you like it bends,
> A Bowline on a bollard is the best of
>   journey's ends.
> And, as long as men are mariners, I
>   think it safe to say,
> This is a thing that never will be done
>   another way."

The Double Bowline

The double form is tied in the same way as the Double Sheet Bend by adding a second turn to the single turn of the Half Hitch (Fig. 121). With synthetic materials the Single Bowline is not completely reliable, and in any circumstances, as in mountaineering where failure means disaster, if the single form is used, a stopper knot should be made in the free end, as recommended by the British Mountaineering Council; or else the double form should be used (Fig. 122). Enthusiasm for the Single Bowline needs toning down:

> The men who classify the knots do not
>   call bowlines 'bends',
> But 'single loops' and 'double loops' the
>   system comprehends;
> And, as long as men are mountaineers,
>   I'm sure it's safe to say:
> "The single form's not safe enough;
>   please tie some other way!"

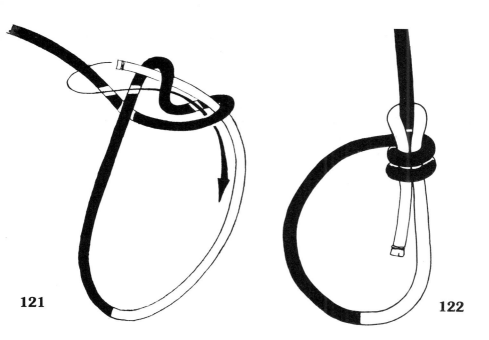

121

122

*The Enhanced Bowline

The rabbit runs north-west behind the tree, east across the front, south-west behind the tree, and then dives down into the burrow (Figs 123 and 124). The two figures show opposite faces of the loop. I offer this variant as an alternative to the Double Bowline.

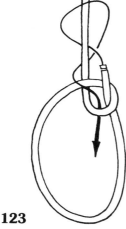

123

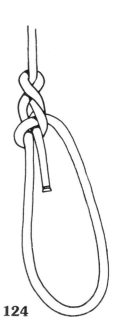

124

*Belt and Braces

The loop is made by *enhancing* a Double Bowline
(Fig. 125), but it is difficult to imagine circumstances which would demand the extra degree of
security.

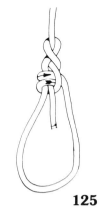

125

Binding Loops

Figure-of-Eight Binding Loop

A Figure-of-Eight knot is tied round the standing
part, as shown (Fig. 126). A good way to start a
parcel.

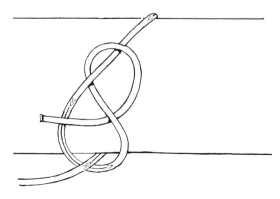

126

Figure-of-Eight Butcher's Knot

This is a knot for rolling a joint, usually a sirloin. Tie the Figure-of-Eight Binding Loop, then make a single hitch in the standing part, and take the running end through it (Fig. 127). There are numerous butcher's knots, but all are finished in this way.

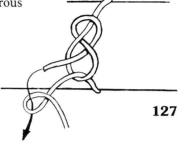

127

Parcel Knot

A skilled exponent ties this knot (Fig. 128) 'flip-flip-flip' in no time at all with the right thumb and forefinger. As you tighten up you get the satisfying feeling that there is just the right amount of friction to allow the smooth sliding action, but also to hold the loop at whatever tension you have set.

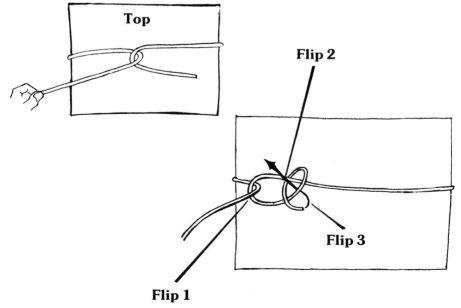

128

Parcel Tying

Start with either of the previously described binding loops, but leave a long end for use at the finish. For a square parcel, start a second loop at right angles to the first, make a Crossing Knot at the back, continue round to the start, and finish with a Half Hitch and a Reef Knot, as shown (Fig. 129). You may need to add to each short end a tight thumb knot pushed closely up against the Reef for extra security (not illustrated).

For a long parcel start with a loop near one end, make Marline Hitches (p.38) down the length, put on Crossing Knots all the way along the back straight, and finish as before.

For the knot to hold well, a twine giving good grip should be used, and *tarred marline* is excellent. With some kinds of string it is only sensible to use sealing wax, or even an adhesive at the final knot.

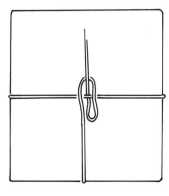

Bottom

129

Top

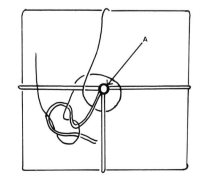

In Fig. 129 'A' represents a binding knot. e.g. Fig. 126 or 128.

Adjustable Loops

Midshipman's Hitch

Tie the loop by making two turns within it and one outside (Fig. 130). All turns are made in the same direction, i.e. pass 'over' the straight part each time. After the knot has been pulled up firmly it can be moved in either direction by a hand placed on it, but otherwise it will remain in the position set and will resist any pull from within the loop. Thus the loop can be set to any desired size, and is a truly remarkable and justly famous knot. It has the same structure as the Rolling Hitch described in Chapter 2. The action is even more reliable if three turns instead of two are made within the loop.

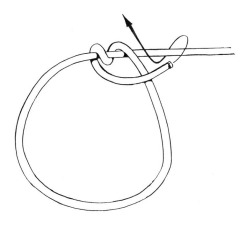

130

The Bowstring Knot

The Honda and Bowstring are really the same knot, but Honda is the term used when it is used as a fixed loop, as in the fixed loop of a lariat, and Bowstring when it is used as an adjustable loop.

Make an overhand knot some way from the end, pass the end round the support, bring it back and take it down through the 'r' space, just as when tying a Honda, but this time there is no need for a stopper knot (Fig. 131). The loop will now resist a pull on the standing part, i.e. no pull on the standing part will cause the loop to lengthen. However, a pull from within the loop on one side will lengthen the loop, and it may readily be untied by this means.

131

The loop was used by the men of yore for fixing one end of the bowstring to the top of the bow. It allowed the string to be lengthened to take the strain off the bow between battles. Nowadays an archer uses a Timber Hitch for the purpose, and if you ask him: "Why not a Bowstring Knot?" he replies: "What's that?"

The knot provides a simple way of controlling the length of a support rope (e.g. a guy rope of a tent, or a tether for an animal).

Loops Tied in the Bight

The Lineman's Loop or Alpine Butterfly Knot

With the right thumb and index 'roll' a left-hand turn (Fig. 132). Hold the turn at the overlap, drop end *A*, seize the loop at *B*, and with it 'roll' the second smaller turn shown in Fig. 133; then pull the whole of the large turn through the small one to form the loop. Fig. 134 shows only the knot at the top of the loop. Figures 133 and 134 show opposite faces. (I thank Mr Lester Copesteak for having discovered this excellent but unusual method of tying, originating in a 1928 number of *The Alpine Journal*.)

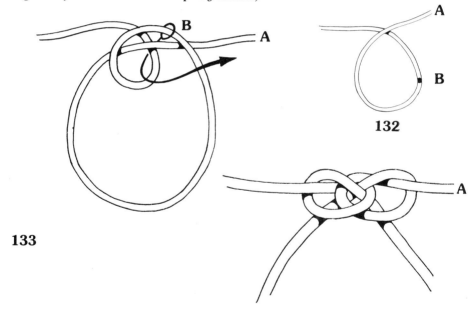

132

133

134

Mountaineers use this loop round the chest, and it is one that is hard to beat for general purposes, being quickly tied, pulling up without the loop shrinking, and breaking readily. Because it is symmetrical it holds equally well whichever end is held. It has the same structure as the Alpine Butterfly *Bend* described in Chapter 4.

The Angler's Loop

This loop (Figs. 135a, 135b and 135c), intended for anglers, is often condemned for use in ropework as prone to jam. Admittedly it is not the easiest knot to break, but it is coming increasingly into general use because, though some time and practice is required to master it, it can be tied extremely quickly in the bight, and it holds well. To learn to tie it with an end, apply the method of Do and Undo. (See page 39.)

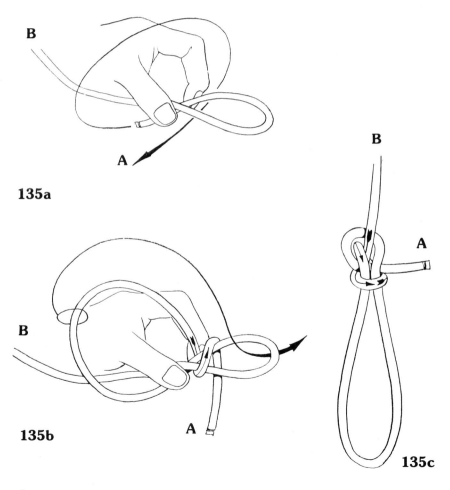

135a

135b

135c

*Loops from Bends

The general method of transforming a bend into a loop is interesting, but as far as I know has never been described. The derivation of the *Corrick Loop* from the *Corrick Bend* will serve as an example.

Start with a loosely tied Corrick bend (p.62) having a long standing part (Fig. 136a). Rearrange the knot by extending the dark running end to form a 'running part' roughly as long as the now shortened standing part (Fig. 136b); and bring the dark running end to abut on the light standing end. If you were to weld these two parts together, a loop of dark and light portions would be formed. Don't do this, but instead take the dark end along the path of the light rope, removing the light rope tuck by tuck as you go, thus forming a Carrick Loop all in one rope. All very simple! (Fig. 136c).

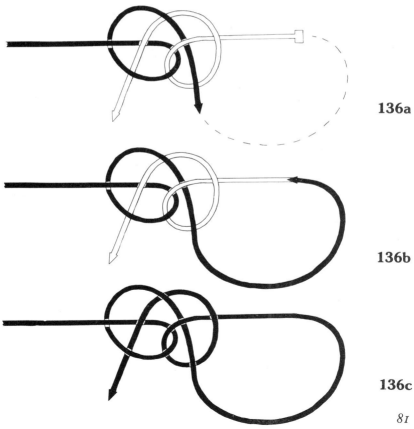

136a

136b

136c

Not all bends yield good loops; the Reef Loop is catastrophic. Bends like Sleeping Beauty (p.65), in which one running end lies parallel to its own standing part, are unlikely to be suitable. The best, but rare, arrangement is where the running end lies parallel to the opposite standing part, as in the Sliding Figure-of-Eight Knot (p.46). Intermediate types such as the Sheet Bend and the Alpine Butterfly Bend can yield good loops. It is a field for the reader to explore.

The loop derived from the Alpine Butterfly Bend will be an *end loop*, which is not the same as the Alpine Butterfly loop described on page 79, where the pull is applied at both ends.

*Bends from Loops

The reverse procedure is vastly simpler. Fig. 137 shows an Angler's Loop (p.80). Evidently if the loop is cut at A it will straighten out to form the standing part of a bend. If the cut is made at B, a somewhat different bend will be formed.

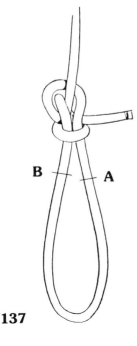

137

Double and Multiple Loop Knots

Bowline on a Bight

Double a length of *limp* rope or cord, and with it start as if to tie an ordinary single Bowline (Fig. 138); then fold a very short length of the closed end back (Fig. 139), pull the whole of the double loop through it and tighten up (Fig. 140). A common way is to pull a large piece through and use it to encircle the double loop, but this method is more likely to lead to a capsize, particularly if the rope is stiff.

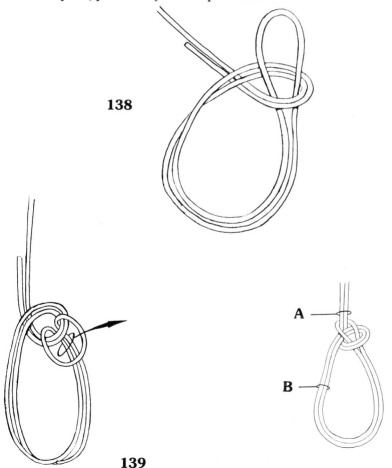

138

139

A

B

140

It is wise to provoke the capsize deliberately. To do so, loosen the completed knot and pull apart portions 'a' and 'b', so straightening out the Half Hitch. A running noose is then produced which could be catastrophic for anyone seated in the loops. Learn to restore the situation.

*Brummycham Bowline

This double loop is chiefly for use when both ends of the rope are available for tying. Make two single turns, drop a half hitch over both at one end (Fig. 141); then take the *standing end* through the space above the hitch (Fig. 142). Adjust the relative size of the loops to requirements, and pull each half of each loop tight (Fig. 143).

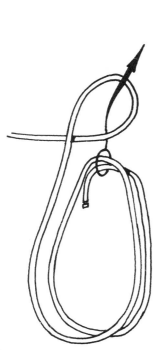

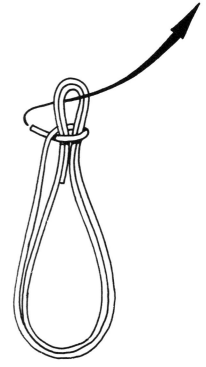

141

142

To learn to tie the knot with one end only, first tie as above with both ends. Next, using the principle of Do and Undo (p.39), untie the knot using the end only, then reverse the procedure.

*Multiple Brummychams

Any number of turns may be made, but more and more care in pulling up is required as the number increases. The method may be applied to secure a skein of rope.

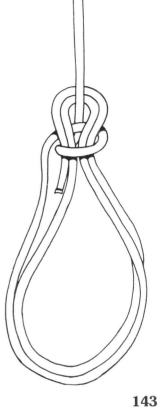

143

The Noose

The Simple Noose

There are two ways to tie it:

(i) Tie an overhand knot round the standing part; or

(ii) Hold the end of the rope in one hand, make a small half hitch with the other, and pull a bight of the standing part through it.

In both methods a stopper knot should be added (Fig. 144). The slipped form of the noose has been described under the title Halter Hitch (p.31).

144

The Honda Lariat

Make a small Honda Loop (p.68) then pull a bight of the standing part through to make the lariat (Fig. 145).

145

Running Bowline

Simply tie a small Bowline Loop round the standing part; or tie a small bowline at the end, and take a bight of the standing part through it (Fig. 146).

146

Applications

Any noose may be used as the first loop in tying up a parcel; it will take the place of the Figure-of-Eight Binding Loop described earlier, and does not have to be of the binding variety.

Nooses form excellent hitches which have two chief uses:

(i) To tie round something large, like a really wide tree trunk, with a noose only one turn is required, and far less rope will be required than with any hitch of more than one turn such as a Clove, Cow, or Constrictor. The Timber Hitch needs one turn only, but then it almost amounts to a noose. Nooses used as hitches are extremely secure.

(ii) To attach a noose to some inaccessible place like the base of a prickly hawthorn hedge or replacing a spinnaker sheet whilst the sail is flying, the end may be passed round the support once only and the rest of the knot can be completed in comfort at a distance from it.

Index

Obtaining Rope

Jimmy Green Marine. The Coachyard, Berryhill, Beer, East Devon EX12 3JP. Tel: Seaton (0297) 20744. Call at this address, or order for free delivery.
Marlow Yacht Ropes. South Road, Hailsham, East Sussex. Tel: 0323 847234. They do not supply retail, but will give the name of your local retail outlet.
Kevin Keatley. 19 Wakehurst Place, Rustington, West Sussex BN16 3NG. Tel: 0903 776092. Goods supplied by post.
Footrope Knots. Des and Liz Pawson, 501 Wherstead Road, Ipswich, Suffolk. Knotting books, tools, materials.
All the firms listed above supply a detailed list with prices on receipt of a stamped addressed envelope.

A more detailed account of the system is given in *A New System of Knotting*, by Dr Harry Asher, published by the International Guild of Knot Tyers and obtainable by post from Mr Frank Harris, 14 Games House, Springfield Grove, Charlton, London SE7 7TN. Price £3.90 inc. p&p.